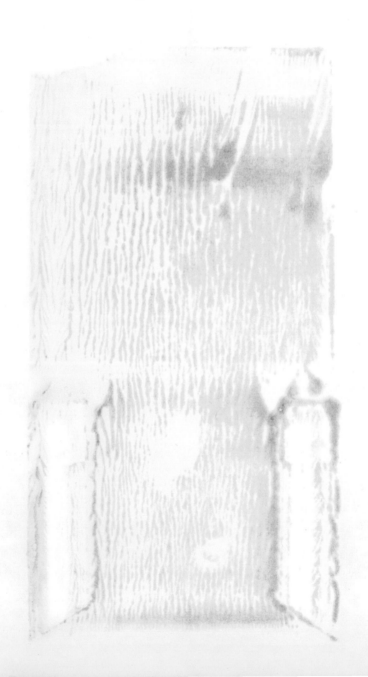

EDUCATION—THEN AND NOW

by

Faye R. McAdoo

DORRANCE & COMPANY

Philadelphia

Dedicated to my two nieces,
Elisa Steenweg Lewis
for
typing the manuscript
and
Gwen Lewis Kunkle
for
illustrating the manuscript

CONTENTS

Page

PREFACE

In this book you are about to read, I wish to tell the reader the advances education has made in the last fifty years. Sometimes we get the idea that education is just standing still marking time, or what have you. I think when you have finished reading this book you will discover that education has made great strides in reaching its present level. It has made tremendous strides in the last decade and many more are anticipated. To mention a few, great achievement has been accomplished in the fields of reading, science, and mathematics. Witness the space age, modern machines, etc.

My educational background includes a B.S. in Education from the Indiana University of Pennsylvania, plus an M.S. in Education from the University of Pittsburgh in Pittsburgh, Pennsylvania, in addition to forty-four years of education experience in all grades from one through eight. I know whereof I speak.

My reasons for taking the time to write this book are that I wish people to know about strides in education and that people sometimes wonder about education in the one-room schools of America thirty or forty years ago. Many famous people started their education in a one-room school and believe me, the teacher made the school ... be it good or mediocre.

Gwen Lewis Kualks

Chapter I

TEACHER PREPARATION

When we applied for a teaching position, we sent our applications to one of the school board members. On an appointed day, the school board, consisting of five men plus the applicants, went to a designated school, usually the school nearest the center of the school district. The board transacted all business concerning the school and then "Let the Schools" was said. These meetings were called "school lettings." After several hours of deliberation, we were called into the presence of a very august board. The secretary of the board read the names of those successful applicants and name of the rural school in which the applicant was to teach the coming school year. We were usually moved around every two years. When the list was read, the applicants not getting hired left and the successful teachers stayed on to sign a contract with the board.

Teacher preparation or qualifications had no consideration here in this procedure. If you were a relative of a board member or came from a prominent family in the community, or were credited with being a strict disciplinarian or were a member of the male sex, you were in.

Chapter II

PHYSICAL PLANT

The physical plant has really undergone a reformation. This is the area where the layman, the person who has little or no information relative to education professionally, can see the changes, from a little one-room wooden school to one of bricks numbering several rooms plus a cafeteria or multiple-purpose room, a gymnasium, a library, a science room, a music room and a darkroom for showing films and slides, a room where the chairs and desks are movable instead of where the desks are screwed to the floor, a room where a pretty scenic picture or pictures hang on the wall versus one of George Washington or Abraham Lincoln (there is nothing wrong with George or Abe, but one does tire of looking at them). The furnishings in the rooms of today's schools are pleasing in color, design and usefulness. In 1924, the desks were too high or sometimes too low for the seat upon which the pupil sat. (I spent a good many hours adjusting seats and desks in my rural schoolrooms.) These desks were usually the double variety and so were occupied by two pupils. This situation led to many quarrels concerning the contents of the desk.

School buildings have grown from approximately 30 feet by 30 feet to something like 660 feet by 400 feet. The school building in Greenford, Ohio, was really larger because it housed everyone from kindergarten through the twelfth grade. This, I thought, was such a good idea. The building contained a cafeteria, library, science room, gymnasium, and offices. If you had a problem with which help was needed, the supervisor was right there. It was really nice to greet the administration day by day.

Instead of the pupils' coming from one small district where

everyone knew everyone else, they came from an area of ten to twenty square miles, or even more. Everyone is bussed to school . . . eliminating hazards of the highway. No one walks. This is a much better arrangement because then the children meet others who may be from an entirely different environment, urban versus rural or rich district versus a disadvantaged district. In 1924, my first school was strictly rural and my last school in Chester, West Virginia, was mixed urban and rural. It was advantageous for the urban and rural pupils to swap experiences. The best example of bussing was at Greenford, Ohio. There the boys and girls from the rich farms thereabouts met with the middle class and wealthy villagers. These people were really considerate and kind to an alien teacher from Pennsylvania.

In 1924, the schoolrooms were not lighted. If we had a program at night, quite a few brought kerosene lanterns. If we were lucky, someone provided a lamp that burned a mixture of gasoline and air and really gave a very good light. Fifty years later, our schoolrooms and school buildings were well lighted with incandescent electric lights. We tried to have all meetings in the daytime because then there wasn't a lighting problem. I recall quite a few times in the winter, especially in December, January and February, storms' coming up and the classroom's getting so dark the children couldn't see to read. At such times, we played games until it brightened up enough to have classes. If it continued to be dark, an early dismissal was in order. How the pupils liked this! Such a situation is unbelievable today.

When it came to heating the schoolroom, one's thoughts become quite nostalgic. In the center of the room was a large stove. It was fired until it glowed red on the outside. Those children sitting too near the heating system were being quite roasted and those farther away were too cold. We used a rotation system until the schoolroom became warm on the outside edges. Those cold and farther away from the stove moved closer and those too close traded with someone farther away.

Although it was quite a community project within our little circle, the teacher provided her own wood to kindle the fire. We asked the board to furnish wood, but were told that some teachers used more wood than others so it was best that the teacher just furnish his or her own wood. I remember going down the road with a bundle of wood under my arm just in case I needed to rekindle the fire. My youngest brother was pretty good at keeping me supplied with kindling wood. Today the schools are heated by steam generated from a large boiler and operated by a man who understands heat. We would have a fifteen minute recess between morning and noon and between noon and dismissal. At this time, we brought in more coal with which to stoke the fire. Some of the larger boys would bring a bucket of coal, but more often than not, the lot fell to the teacher.

It was necessary to get to school early in the winter in order to get a fire going and to heat the schoolroom. These farmers got up early because they were dairy farmers and had work to do. So the children were on their way to school early, too. I remember thawing out a good many frostbitten fingers and toes. One morning, as I recall, with the temperature at minus ten degrees, a little girl came in crying with cold toes. She had no socks in her shoes. Her toes were really stinging. I sent her to a very good friend and helper of mine, a very kind lady, to get her warmed up and comfortable. She kept her until she was quite over the chill cold and then allowed her to return to school. This lady was always hunting up socks and mittens for the children.

The health facilities in 1924 were really something! Outdoor toilets, one for the boys and one for the girls, were often located 200 or 300 feet from the schoolhouse. Needless to say, no more trips than necessary were made in the wintertime. During the summer, the toilets were well disinfected! They were given a handful of hydrated lime! The schoolroom was equally well cared for. Sometime before school began in September, the floor was oiled with some crude coal oil. I never quite knew what this was to do. I just knew that unless I was going to walk home (which I usually did) my shoes were left in the schoolroom and another pair worn home. My mother wouldn't let me in the house in my coal oil shoes.

Personal hygiene was the unknown factor in 1924. To wash their hands at school was quite a feat for the children. There was one common basin for the entire school. Quite frequently the hands were washed at the source of water supply! Since towels were never furnished I asked each pupil to bring his or her own towel. This was not always done. Often they washed their hands and then flung the hands around until they were dry.

The water supply was quite another situation. Most of the schools had a spring of water nearby. My first school in 1924 was supplied by a spring which bubbled out of the hill. Most children preferred to drink by lying down and putting their faces into the water. Not many of the children bothered to get a drinking cup. Those that did used the containers in their lunch boxes.

One of the memories I cherish most was about our cafeteria. One rural school where I taught had seventy percent of the pupils underweight. When the county school nurse weighed them, that was her finding. She was aghast, and so was I. I just didn't know why this had to be because the children came from farms where there were plenty of fruits, vegetables and dairy products. I consulted with our home economics adviser for the county. She thought this a good project for a Lunch Box Club. Immediately we organized just such a club. The children really liked this club. The mothers were very cooperative. The club went like this. In the evening, a small jar of food ... leftovers ... was filled from the dinner meal ... maybe stew, tomatoes, soup, baked beans, etc. It was really quite a conglomeration of food! This jar was put in the lunch box the next morning. At recess time, a large flat pan was partially filled with water and put on the top of the stove. All the jars were put into the pan of water and by noon they were heated through and ready to be eaten along with the sandwiches in the lunch boxes.

When spring came, we had an official weigh in and the seventy percent in the fall was now down to thirty-five percent with not as much weight deficiency as in the autumn. The lunches were more enjoyable since a hot food was now available. And the children waited eagerly for the home economics representative to come ... she was young, pretty, and quite exuberant in her praise for the children. She was so pleased with the experiment that she had me go before a group of farm mothers in the county and tell the results of the venture. I, too, was pleased since the children were more educable than before, not nearly so listless and tired. One sad note in the club was when a little boy lost his mother and said he'd have to give up the club. The teacher and children saw to it that he had his warm jar of food each day. This caused the club to really appreciate their homes and mothers when they realized the effect on their classmate. This group was a fine bunch of children and one I have really enjoyed when going back into my memories ... the Lunch Box Club.

In 1924 we were called to order by the school bell ... not a buzzer. The bell was rung religiously at 8:30 A.M. for the children to leave home for school ... at 9:00 for school to begin ... at 12:45 for the children to get a drink, go to the toilet and get ready for school ... at 1:00 for school to begin in the afternoon. Many people listened for the school bell. To many people it brought back memories of their school days. Once in a while it would be possible to hear the bell of another district ring.

The schools in my district were kept painted, white outside and inside. Then a short time after the Great Depression, electricity came to the country. The schools were furnished with electricity. This was a real boon to the country school.

The school board consisted of five members and each one looked after the repairs of the school in which he resided ... replacing glass, mowing the grass, repairing the stove, etc.

In the matter of supplies, each teacher got his or her own. The supplies were kept at the secretary's home. You just went and secured your own from what was on the shelves. When it came to textbooks . . . the secretary of the school board, or a board member selected them. The teachers were not consulted. It was rumored that the secretary was quite often bribed into selecting the text the agent was selling. This arrangement worked out fine for the secretary, and the agent selling the books . . . but the child and teacher had to make the best of it sometimes.

In one rural school where I taught, we had a bus system. A school was closed and the children were bussed to Grant School. One year a lady transported the children. They had a distance of about three miles to travel one way. She traveled over a clay road. In the winter and spring the road was almost impassable, hub-deep with mud. Not much help was given to her by the road supervisors. This lady drove a team of horses and a wagon during the bad weather. During the nice weather she drove a car. She averaged six to eight children daily. The children liked her very much and had a lot of fun during the daily travels. She was a big-hearted person, very congenial, and with a fun-loving disposition. I recall once when I got storm-stayed she sent me over a tray of warm and very delicious food. (She lived in view of the schoolhouse.) She took off her boots and lent them to me to get home. I thoroughly enjoyed working with this particular bus driver.

So we went from a wagon or surrey with the fringe on top in 1924, to the warm motor-driven busses of today. A few of today's busses have educational films for viewing while the children ride to and from school.

Chapter III

TEACHER TRAVEL

My first year in teaching I walked a distance of three miles over the highest ridge in Indiana County, Pennsylvania. It was a steady climb for about one and a half miles before I reached the top of the ridge. Upon reaching the top I was ready to rest. In the quiet of the top of the ridge I could ponder many things. I often thought about my pupils, their home background, their aims for life, their capabilities and their incapabilities. It was on the top of this ridge that I made up any lesson plans for the day sitting on a zig-zag rail fence. I couldn't have found a more serene or scenic spot to think about what I was going to do that day. I thought of what I was going to do for my boys and girls ranging in age from six years to fifteen years, their varying needs and personalities. Many problems in my first year of teaching were pondered and solved while sitting on farmer Brown's rail fence.

Chapter IV

COURSE OF STUDY

In 1924, the course of study included those subjects necessary for a well-rounded education in an agrarian society . . . reading, spelling, English, mathematics (including algebra for the eighth graders) geography, history, civics and handwriting. Then came the year 1969-70. Science was most necessary. It had been added quite a few years previous to 1969-70. Science was stressed in the curriculum following World War II. Algebra was dropped as such from the elementary curriculum. Along with the addition of science came music, art and physical education. The regular homeroom teachers in the rural school of 1924 did not include music and art as such in their teaching. In 1924, the rural teacher was "it." He or she taught everything including music, art, science, and physical education plus library science.

What a time I had in teaching music, being a monotone. Usually one of the elder pupils would be able to lead the singing. Being able to play the organ I knew when the music was sung correctly. Following World War II came an age of centralization when one-room schools were closed down and good, consolidated schools with modern facilities were erected in their places. Most children now had a school better than their homes. With the close of World War II came an age of specialization in which the teachers got some help. They were no longer it. They taught only a few subjects and were able to do a much better job of their teaching. There came help in music, art, physical education and science. Most schools had a writing supervisor to help the teachers in this area.

All told, the educational process was going into an age of specialization. The administrative staff realized that teachers were not specialists in all fields of education. This, in turn, has been a great help to teachers. As I previously stated, I was a monotone and greatly relished the help in music. This has given students a more diverse and better-rounded education in the special fields. Students talented in art, music or science could develop their careers in fields in which they were interested or had talent under the guidance of specialists.

Chapter V

TEACHERS' SALARIES

In 1924, a school year was seven and a half months. The salary paid was sixty-eight dollars per month. We were paid this amount by check and I must say it was paid promptly. There were no paydays during the summer—we were just turned out to pasture. We had to save enough during the winter to go to school during the summer and pay any other expenses we might incur. Usually we started in in September with a deficit. Those were the good old days! When I retired in 1969, in West Virginia, I was making, within a few dollars of that amount per day. We were required by law to spend one week at a county institute . . . five days and four nights. We supposedly were cultured from the night programs. Usually one night was an opera. The teachers in my district, including myself, didn't know the story in the opera and so not much was gotten out of it. We didn't know anything more about opera than a pig would know about Sunday. Usually one of the night attractions would be a play. Then the other two nights would be a lecture and "mixed pickles." We were paid twenty dollars for our attendance at the institute. This constituted a real boon to our meager budget.

About ten years later, our salaries were increased to $100.00 per month with an eight-month term. This was enacted into law by the Pennsylvania General Assembly. However, when a Republican became governor of Pennsylvania, our salaries were cut to $90.00. This governor even wanted to dip into the pension fund set up by the retirement board. This he could not do, because each member's account is like a bank account in the individual's name. Later that year, the cut from $100.00 to $90.00 was restored by the General Assembly. We were to have

11

the cut added to our pay, but due to some finagling by our school board we never received the restored money. No teacher was willing to try to force our board to pay it. It could have meant the job of that particular teacher. My assistant superintendent from the county office suggested that I write to Harrisburg, the capital, about the cut, and request them to advise our board to restore the same deductions to our teachers. I did just that but nothing came of it. Our teaching jobs were very precarious. If we became ill the school was closed down until we could get back to the job. One teacher I knew paid her own substitute while she was absent during the death and funeral of her father. I suggested to one of my neighbors, a school board member, that this was not right. His reply, "She selected her own substitute and so was liable for the pay." We never heard of fringe benefits, as there weren't any.

Today's teachers are guaranteed wages of $6,000 state minimum. I'm submitting a chart to show wages paid to teachers as of April, 1969.

During the interim from 1924 to 1969, salaries increased from $680.00 to $6,000.00. Sick leave was granted in the amount of ten days a year and now the unused sick leave can be transferred to another school district. Most school districts give two or three days for personal use, and one day with no questions asked. Some districts allow their teachers to attend educational conferences without loss of pay. Along with the demands for more training came more remuneration for the teaching profession. Today's teachers have to come from homes and farms where more money can be set aside for education than was the case in 1924. You finished eighth grade and then went to summer school for nine or twelve weeks and were given a teaching certificate; today, you must finish high school then attain a degree in a college or university to be issued a teaching certificate. Therefore, it is a different group economically than in 1924, and producing a scarcity of teachers. If the teacher doesn't really want to dedicate himself or herself to the job as an educator, then he or she shouldn't waste four years in the educational field to become a teacher. A child can spot a phony as far down the hall as he can see him coming. I would never for one fleeting moment give up the experience I had in the classrooms of this tri-state area.

Then came the idea of merit pay. We all realize that the best, most dedicated teachers are worth more, and should be rewarded more than the teachers who are only using education as a stopgap until something more rewarding comes along. Teachers themselves make merit ratings of their co-workers. When it is time to select a member for a special assignment, it goes to the career teacher, because teachers themselves want to be sure to present a good picture to the public. When someone is advanced to a supervisory position, the teachers themselves select a superior teacher. But in the matter of salary, teachers do not like merit pay. I, for one, would not like to teach where one teacher could be selected as an outstanding teacher and receive more pay than I. I'd not want to be selected as the one outstanding teacher, nor would I want not to be selected at all. Either way, any teacher would feel highly embarrassed among his or her fellow teachers. I think merit pay would be fine if you set up hurdles or goals to be attained, for instance, more education, travel or some school project that would be of benefit to the group in a school. If there were no guidelines, the teachers' efforts would be directed inward toward themselves and not toward any learning process. Then merit pay would defeat the best efforts to improve the educational status of the students, the school and the community. Much bitterness, envy and enmity could result where there were no guidelines for merit ratings.

Chapter VI

TEACHER SUPERVISION

Teacher supervision. Now that was something! In the rural areas the supervision was done by the board of directors. This board consisted of five men. These five men were citizens of the community who would take time out to do their civic duty. They were chosen by the voters of the district for a term of six years. They had to have no educational qualifications. Some of them wanted to serve because they had an axe to grind. About the only time the board came to life was at school letting time. They listened to the citizens of each district tell what teacher they wanted or didn't want. They didn't necessarily need to be educated in school affairs. Teacher qualifications had no place in this scheme of things. I well remember my first year of teaching and meeting one of the directors and his telling me I was to dismiss grades one, two and three early, or just when I got them excited. These directors were directing teachers with many more years of education than they. They were the prominent citizens of the district with good common sense, and I suppose that was their stock in trade. We were also supervised by the county superintendent and his assistant. The county superintendent came once a year, and the assistant superintendent came twice a year. They would stay approximately a half hour. What teacher couldn't fool a supervisor for a half hour? That was the supervision fifty years ago! If you weren't liked by a citizen in your district you likely wouldn't be hired. There was no tenure. I never could teach in my home school because our board secretary listened to a lady who did not like me.

I know of one teacher who lost her job because she let a boy's dog lie behind the stove in her classroom on a sub-zero winter day. Today's teachers are protected by tenure, and not by some board member who does not happen to like dogs.

If a teacher in 1924 traveled outside the community, it was best not to advertise the fact. Teachers just weren't supposed to be paid wages to enable them to travel. How times have changed! Today administrators like their teachers to travel. New ideas are introduced into the classroom. New ideas are gathered by teachers visiting teachers from other states and other countries.

In 1924, teachers usually stayed pretty close to home base; not so today. In 1924, teachers usually walked to school, even in the most inclement weather. I well remember walking in snow two and three feet deep. I have walked four and five miles to school. I knew all the shortcuts to get to school. Now as I look back to those days of walking I'm reminded of a walk I frequently used when the roads were impassable. I crossed a stream about twenty feet wide and during the winter season this stream carried a large volume of water. I crossed this stream on a tree that had fallen across it. When the tree was frozen with rain, or was snow-covered this was especially hazardous, as I would have fallen four or five feet into icy water three or four feet deep. Then I journeyed across a pasture into the woods. About the time I entered the woods, day was breaking. More than once I was startled by a herd of deer. I knew they were near, but I was so busy with my own thoughts I'd forget them. I usually saw them on my way across the ridge. Then on the other side of the ridge I'd take a shortcut across a farmer's field. This farmer's wife frequently wanted me to stay the night. I sometimes did stay. She made the best bean soup I've ever eaten. When I'd stay to spend the night, which I frequently did, she would talk late into the night and I'm pretty much of a sleepy-head. The parents of this school also wanted me to stay quite frequently; they vied with each other to see who could put the most food on the table. The food was so delectable and so attractively served, I'd always end up by eating too much. To me they were the world's best patrons and I loved every one of them. They were so cooperative and always looking for ways to do something for their teacher.

In 1926 I bought a Model T Ford which my youngest brother liked to drive. Just as soon as the roads were passable in the spring, he would come for me in the evening to take me home. One evening he decided the roads were passable and started out to bring me home. He mired the car up to the axles. I had to get a farmer to dig the car out. He was wedged between two logs from an old corduroy road. Well, such was the situation in the early twenties and thirties.

Today teachers drive twenty and thirty miles to reach the school where they work. While teaching in Ohio, 1 drove thirty miles over improved highway in the sixties. The car I used was much improved over the car I used in the twenties. I pushed uphill with my right foot (a model A Ford); in the car I used in the sixties, I floated uphill and down in air-conditioned comfort.

Chapter VII

MACHINES IN THE CLASSROOM

In 1924 the schoolroom in which I found myself did not have anything mechanical . . . not even a pencil sharpener.

I very clearly remember asking a member of the board of education for a pencil sharpener. His reply was that they were not furnished by the board, just use a boy's knife. Many times I bought my own art paper since the kind I wanted was not furnished. Today the schoolroom has many mechanical tools to be used education-wise. A film can be obtained from the school's learning center for almost everything that is to be taught. There are machines which the students can operate to help themselves better understand a point stressed. Many, many machines are available to help the teacher and students grasp the information studied.

I distinctly remember a machine I used in Greenford, Ohio. The teacher could put the child's work on the projector. Then the work was magnified many times on an overhead screen. From this it was easy to point out where a definite set of rules for punctuation, sentence structure or capitalization was needed. The whole class could and did participate in the discussion. Needless to say, I had one hundred percent participation. The names, of course, were blotted out on each paper. The next lesson was a repeat and what a difference there was in the paper. What a difference! In 1924 in my wildest imaginings I would not have thought of a machine such as this!

Then there are duplicating machines today to duplicate any materials necessary for the job at hand. Just load them up and press a button, and you can get as many copies as you need. Machines such as Xerox, thermofax, and duplicating machines, both mechanical and electrical, are on the education market.

I well remember the first duplicating machine I used. I borrowed my mother's cookie sheet and filled it with gelatin. Next I bought a pencil to make a master copy. Then put the copy face down on the gelatin until it would transfer. The copies were better than none at all . . . but they left much to be desired. There were places where they were too dark, too light and places where there was no copy at all. They did serve a purpose . . . more drill in a more interesting way.

Today we can make a master copy and have it transferred to usable material in a matter of minutes. We have tape recorders which we can use to help students who have missed out on the regular presentation of the subject catch up. We have slide projectors, overhead projectors and opaque projectors.

I taught fifth and sixth grades in English, spelling, and geography in my later years of teaching. On one of my trips to Washington State we took slides in every state. We have some beautiful slides of the Central Plains, Great Plains, Plateau states and Rocky Mountain states, the Columbian Plateau, and numerous valleys in between. We have slides of Independence, Rio, Yellowstone, Springfield, Illinois (Lincoln land), Bad Lands, Black Hills, Tetons, and last but not the least, Glacier Park. One day I was showing my trip across the U.S. and we got out to Washington State. The children wouldn't let me alone until I brought them back. I'm sure when I mentioned Bad Lands . . . land too worthless for anything . . . Tetons, mountains not worn down . . . glaciers, geysers, hot springs, valleys, reservations, and mile upon mile of corn in the Central Plains and mile upon mile of wheat in the Columbian plateau, they all had mental pictures of what I was talking about. We came home through the Indian reservations and got many good pictures of Indian life. We came through Paul Bunyan territory at Bemidji, Minnesota. When I talked about the lakes in Minnesota I'm sure my class had a mental image of Minnesota's 10,000 lakes.

I would be sure to use my slides from other regions I have visited . . . New York City, fruit belt of New York along Lake

Plains, Washington, D.C., and Florida, to mention a few. And just because the teacher took the slides and explained them made them more interesting.

I must not forget the plastic maps of today, maps where the students can touch high and higher elevations of land, and can also see low elevations. When I compare the black and white maps with the plastic maps . . . what a difference in the pupils' being able to see elevation.

Today most schools have a learning resource center, a center which has everything to make teaching easier. From the center you can get special books, diagrams, slides, cassettes, and even models of the things that you are studying.

Today when I go into a modern classroom and see the rows upon rows of prettily illustrated books all the way from kindergarten, through twelfth grade, I can't help but think of my 1924 classroom. In that 1924 classroom we had *Webster's Dictionary, Arabian Nights* and *Vanity Fair*. These books were for first grade to eighth grade.

In our modern classrooms of today we have some pupils who will be listening to a record on earphones, while another pupil in the same classroom will be viewing slides, and still others may be studying diagrams and others reading. The teacher will be answering questions.

The pacer is a good device used by many first grade teachers. It can be used from first through twelfth grade. The pacer is set to develop speed in reading. Its principal use is in junior high school to develop speed in reading. I remember watching a class in seventh grade in Greenfield, Ohio, doing a reading lesson on the pacer. They found the pacer quite interesting. Since they had been my pupils the previous year, they wanted me to try the pacer. The material was on *Lorna Doone*. I was quite familiar with the material and as a result I beat the pacer. The instructor decided the material was too easy for me.

A most recent development by Bell Telephone and AT&T has been to make courses readily available to high schools where a few students need the course. Recently a high school had a very few students that needed courses in chemistry and Latin, but it was not worthwhile to add a faculty member. So Bell and AT&T came to the rescue. They installed a loud-speaker for listening, and microphones for asking questions. The machines could be plugged into any phone jack or electrical outlet. The instructor could have many pupils in different schools. These proved very worthwhile.

Today nurses can make use of machines to guide the pupils' health. There is the audiometer for hearing, charts for determining deficiencies in eyesight. Goodness knows, parents need help in determining the eye and ear defects in their children.

When I think of my classroom in 1924 and compare it with today's classroom—no machines in 1924 and the classroom of today with numberless machines, charts, slides, diagrams, ditto machines, and row after row of books prettily illustrated—I know that education has come a long way and will still go a long way with today's leaders.

We have come a long way on many devices and new tools of learning. We probably have only scratched the surface.

Chapter VIII

TEACHER'S STATUS IN OTHER PROFESSIONS

The teacher's status in the community has come a long way since the days of Ichabod Crane. I'm not sure whether Washington Irving did the teachers a service or disservice by putting Ichabod in such a ridiculous plight. I'm inclined to think it was a service because I don't believe we have any Ichabods in the teaching profession today.

In 1924 when this story began, teachers were tied to the economic and social status associated with the middle class agrarians. If a teacher tried to rise above that category, he or she was in immediate trouble. One teacher I know lost her job because she acquired a fur coat and the district school board wives couldn't afford a fur coat. Teachers for the most part drove used cars or the cheapest model obtainable because after all, that was about all they could afford. (I still get a guilty feeling when I buy a car today.) If you went on a vacation of even a week's duration you kept quiet about it because the people who managed the schools didn't go on vacations. How this has all been changed!

Today teachers dress in what pleases them with no thought of a school board's approval. They dress like the people of the community and wear what becomes them with no thoughts of acceptance from any group. The automobiles they own are of their own choosing. As for vacations, they are world travelers. In fact, school administrators are glad to hear they have been on vacations outside of their own back yard. Many teachers today go jaunting off to Europe on a minute's notice. Some go during vacations.

In 1924, teachers not only taught school, but were coerced into heading up all kinds of drives in the community. They were expected to take part in all church and community social activities. Most community organizations were frequently organized by teachers. If one taught out of his or her respective community, he was not supposed to be a "suitcase" teacher but was expected to spend weekends in the community doing whatever was necessary for the betterment and progressiveness of the community. Teachers had better not be caught doing what some members of the community might not think was for its betterment. One teacher I know lost her job because she went square dancing.

During the Great Depression years, married women were not supposed to be teaching. The teaching jobs were for men and single girls. Many editorials were written condemning married women in the classrooms. It mattered not how efficiently or how well the married women could teach. I never could understand why saying "I Do" caused a woman teacher to suddenly lose her proficiency as an educator, but to many school boards this was suddenly the case. As a result, some teachers tried to hide the fact that they were married. To me, this situation was all wrong. It cost as much for a married woman to get her education as for a single girl. If the married teacher had something to offer her community she should not have been discriminated against. I've never felt that our schools should be run on a charitable basis, but if a teacher had something to offer her community and that community needed her, then she should have had the position regardless of marital status. If a teacher whose aim was to teach appeared, then that teacher should have been heading up the school.

Then along came World War II and the married teacher was again desperately needed in the classrooms. They came back in large numbers to help alleviate the teacher shortage. Many stayed on after the war because there was a continuing shortage of teachers. The standards for entering teaching were made higher and thus the shortage was created.

To sum up the status of the teachers in the community, let's say they have gone from Irving's idiotic sarcasm heaped upon

Ichabod Crane to becoming leaders in the world of music, art, science, politics, etc. We can be extremely glad to say, "I'm a teacher," "I was a teacher," "I'm a retired teacher," and to become associated with individual, community and world movements for the betterment of mankind.

After teaching for twenty years, I decided to go into an urban school. First because the salary was better, and secondly I was just following a teacher whose skills I did not approve of, and wanted to stop the merry-go-round. Upon reaching an urban school, I was assigned to seventh and eighth grades, teaching reading, spelling, math, and geography. And incidentally, I taught in this same school and same room until I retired from Pennsylvania schools seventeen years later.

One day my supervisor from Pittsburgh came into my room to observe me. After listening to a seventh grade reading lesson he said "Why don't you get your degree? I should think you'd want it. You are doing a good job now, but how much better you'd do with more education." That set me to thinking and I decided to go back to school and get my degree in Elementary Education. Two years later I graduated with a B.S. in Education from Indiana University of Pennsylvania (then known as Indiana State Teachers' College). I had more confidence in my ability to teach and much more understanding of the children I was teaching. First, I had a number of methods courses which enabled me to know what decisions to make and usually how to make them much more justly. And believe me, the courses came in very handy because there were many quarrels to solve and many problems to decide. Secondly, in the community there would be old quarrels and these found their way into the school. There were many facets of life to be dealt with in a rural community . . . births, deaths, old quarrels, weddings, politics, etc. One soon learned to keep out of things not relevant to education. Thirdly, the methods courses were a real help in knowing what to do, when to do it and how.

The requirements for a teacher in Pennsylvania in 1924 were quite mediocre, but I was surely very confident that I could

Effective with September School Openings

PSEA's New State Mandated Schedule

	A	B	C	D	E	F	G	H	I	J	K	L	M	N	O	P
13	9300	9600	9500	9800	10550											10850
12	9300	9300	9500	9500	10550											10550
11	9000	9000	9200	9200	10250	11550	12050	12550	13050	13550	14350	14850	15350	15850	16350	10250
10	8700	8700	8900	8900	9950	11250	11750	12250	12750	13250	14050	14550	15050	15550	16050	9950
9	8400	8400	8600	8600	9650	10950	11450	11950	12450	12950	13750	14250	14750	15250	15750	9650
8	8100	8100	8300	8300	9350	10550	11050	11550	12050	12550	13250	13750	14250	14750	15250	9350
7	7800	7800	8000	8000	9050	10150	10650	11150	11650	12150	12750	13250	13750	14250	14750	9050
6	7500	7500	7700	7700	8750	9750	10250	10750	11250	11750	12250	12750	13250	13750	14250	8750
5	7200	7200	7400	7400	8450	9350	9850	10350	10850	11350	11750	12250	12750	13250	13750	8450
4	6900	6900	7100	7100	8150	8950	9450	9950	10450	10950	11250	11750	12250	12750	13250	8150
3	6600	6600	6800	6800	7850	8550	9050	9550	10050	10550	10750	11250	11750	12250	12750	7850
2	6300	6300	6500	6500	7550	8150	8650	9150	9650	10150	10250	10750	11250	11750	12250	7550
1	6000	6000	6200	6200	7250	7750	8250	8750	9250	9750	9750	10250	10750	11250	11750	7250

Professional employes or temporary professional employes, holding a Master's degree or its equivalent, shall receive two additional $300 steps beyond the steps provided herein for holders of a College certificate. The holder of a Master's degree must be placed at least one step higher on the salary schedule than an employe holding only a Bachelor's degree and with the same years of service within the district.

teach boys and girls ranging in age from six to fifteen years in the grades of one through eight. How presumptuous I was I never learned until years later. But the real tragedy was that no other teacher was any better equipped for the task, nor less confident than I. I seldom saw any other teachers and if I did they were no better able to help me professionally because they were as ill equipped and inexperienced as I. My supervisor from the county superintendent's office came twice a year to see all the teachers in the district. He could not come more often, because he had too many teachers to supervise in the county. When he did come, I had too many problems to even single out one to discuss with him.

If a teacher had eighty credits from the local normal school, he or she was regarded as being highly educated. One of our teachers in the district did graduate from the three-year course and she was considered to be quite adequately prepared. I felt my inadequacy as a teacher and my inefficiency as I looked into the faces of my students. There I saw the problems, frustrations and desire to learn as well as the answers I did not have.

Every summer I kept adding credits to my certificate until I had eighty. Then I was given a life license to teach in the state of Pennsylvania. I attended summer classes and night classes when feasible. It was a law that you had to keep adding credits to your certificate until you had eighty. How little I knew about my profession!

Then after getting my B.S. in Education I had a desire to know more about my job and to get more know-how, so I immediately enrolled at the University of Pittsburgh. I graduated three years later with an M.S. in Education. Unquestionably, my first advice for any future teacher would be "Get all the preparation you can for your job." I've never regretted the time nor money I spent to improve my preparation for teaching. How much more understanding I had of my job, my pupils, my supervisor, and administrators. After getting my two degrees in education I was able to stand a little taller! I had more understanding of my job. I had much more confidence not only in myself, but in my supervisors as well. I had the feeling my supervisors knew their job, and were there to help me do a finer job.

In the forty years since I began teaching, preparation for the position has gone from twelve credits in the normal school to a must in having a bachelor's degree in Education plus twenty-four credits for renewal of the certificate beyond the degree. Today special certificates are issued in special fields . . . music, a degree in music; physical education, a degree in physical education; in art, special preparation in art; reading, special reading supervisors, reading consultants; nursing, a degree in nursing; plus many special workers in other fields. When I began in 1924, no one came in to help us out in anything . . . there were no special fields. We were it. Teaching has gone from a surplus of teachers, to a shortage of teachers to a surplus of teachers again . . . from meagerly equipped teachers to highly skilled teachers . . . from conscientious teachers to teachers who couldn't care less.

Chapter IX

REFLECTIONS 1925-1970

Now that I have reached retirement and am living in my Pennsylvania farm home I can look back on many changes in education in my lifetime. But I'm sure that the next fifty years will bring many more changes and some just as startling as that going from a one-room school with no machines to one of several rooms with many machines. When I reflect on my first school with no machines to the classroom in Greenford, Ohio, to one of many machines, I am indeed impressed with education in the fifty years as I knew it. I think that in the next fifty years we will see more machines being introduced into the average classroom. Pupils and students will be able to supplement the knowledge given by the teacher with more and more supplemental material and an enrichment program in which the student can learn things on his own. The student can find out the how, why and what of material he is learning about.

I well remember a composition lesson we had in fifth grade in Greenford, Ohio. The pupils wrote their compositions ... then I read and corrected them. The compositions were returned to them ... they were to remove their names. Then the compositions were flashed on a screen and the whole class could benefit by the corrections. I didn't lose the interest of one pupil during the lesson. Papers were returned to owners and rewritten ... wonderful results! In my wildest imaginings I'd never have dreamed of anything like this fifty years ago.

I think parents will get more involved in school activities with their children. Not just a P.T.A. where the parent and teacher see each other once a month, drink a cup of coffee and eat a cookie, but where plans are evolved and what is best for the child is discussed . . . where problems of the child are given consideration. Parents will see results of tests and measurements on their child, benefit by the education and experience of the teacher, then by discussion of the child, reach a better conclusion.

I think the classroom of the future will be larger. The child will progress at his own rate and will be able to benefit by an enrichment program. In fact, we have many schools under this plan now. The teacher will direct instead of teach . . . machines will be available. Models and books on the subject will also be available. The pupil will not be held back by someone who does not wish to learn, or doesn't want to progress in any one field. There the pupil will achieve success in what he wishes to know more about. The child who is interested in science will find books, models, etc. on science; the child interested in music will find books, records, etc. in music; the child interested in literature, history or what-not can find help on those subjects . . . all independent of the teacher. The teacher's role will be more selective, guiding and advising as well as teaching. Team teaching will enable the pupil to get the benefit of teachers' working on subjects for which the teacher finds a liking . . . not teaching the subject because he or she must.

Lastly, the best thing that has come out of the past fifty years' struggle has been a unified dues system . . . where you must join all organizations or none. As long as we have such people in A.E.A, it will progress and teachers will go on to achieve lasting results. Then the state level in Pennsylvania has good leaders, too, all inspirational leaders urging teachers on to greater things. Then on the local level I have had the benefit of fine supervision: Mr. Taughinbaugh, Mr. Bailey, Mr. Allison. They gave me many ideas on how to teach and with the teaching profession in their hands we can go nowhere else but ahead.

I think teachers, next to the good Lord Himself, can help us to bring about a better world. In my estimation, teachers are the most important people in the world, state, and locality. We must listen, aid and direct each movement that benefits mankind. We must help all we can to make a better place for the child to come into, a more peaceful world. I'm glad to say I helped over the past fifty years. I can't envision the progress of education in the next fifty years, but I'm sure it is in good hands ... we do have dedicated teachers who will bring about just as many changes in the next fifty years.